Wolf Hill

The Copper Cockerel

Roderick Hunt

Illustrated by Alex Brychta

Oxford University Press

OXFORD
UNIVERSITY PRESS

Great Clarendon Street, Oxford OX2 6DP

Oxford New York

Athens Auckland Bangkok Bogotá Buenos Aires Calcutta
Cape Town Chennai Dar es Salaam Delhi Florence Hong Kong Istanbul
Karachi Kuala Lumpur Madrid Melbourne Mexico City Mumbai
Nairobi Paris São Paulo Singapore Taipei Tokyo Toronto Warsaw

and associated companies in Berlin Ibadan

Oxford is a registered trade mark of Oxford University Press

Printed in Hong Kong

Chapter 1

Mr Saffrey smiled at everyone. He locked his fingers together. Then he pushed his arms outwards. His fingers clicked when he did this.

'Click' went Mr Saffrey's fingers.

'Miss Teal's class has done some good work,' said Mr Saffrey. 'It was a project on the sun.'

Everyone in Miss Teal's class looked pleased. It had been a good project.

Mr Saffrey went on. 'The project gave me an idea. We're going to get solar panels. This way the school can help the environment.'

Most of the children looked blank. 'Does anyone know what solar panels are?' asked Mr Saffrey.

Andy put his hand up. 'Yes, Andy?' said Mr Saffrey.

'Solar panels heat up water,' Andy said. 'They use the sun's rays to make the water hot.'

'Yes,' said Mr Saffrey. 'The panels will go on the school roof. They will heat the water for the school.'

The solar panels caused a lot of trouble. They put Kat and her brother Arjo in danger.

Chapter 2

On Friday a lorry came to school. There were scaffolding poles on the back. Mr Saffrey came into the playground. He made the children keep well away.

'The solar panels are coming next week,' said Mr Saffrey. 'That's why the scaffolding has come today.'

Mr Saffrey pointed at the school roof. 'The panels will go there,' he said.

Miss Teal's class stayed out in the playground. 'You can watch the scaffolding go up,' she said. 'You can watch what happens.'

'I hope we don't have to write about this,' said Michael Ward.

After a while, Miss Teal took everyone back to the classroom. 'I want you to do some writing,' she said.

'Here it comes!' hissed Michael Ward.

'It had better not be a poem about scaffolding poles,' Kat said to Najma.

'We're going to write an animal story,' said Miss Teal.

'Thank goodness,' whispered Kat.

'I've an idea for a story,' joked Najma. 'A cat gets stuck on some scaffolding.'

Kat laughed, so Miss Teal made her sit by herself.

Chapter 3

On Monday, Najma called for Kat and Arjo. At school, something was wrong.

A police car was in the playground. Children were standing in groups. Everyone was looking up at something.

Gizmo ran up. His eyes looked wide behind his big glasses. He pointed at the school roof. 'Have you seen it?' he asked.

Kat gasped. 'I can't believe it,' she said. 'The copper cockerel has been stolen again. This is the second time.'

The roof was a mess. The thieves hadn't just taken the cockerel. All the lead had gone. So had all the tiles that ran along the ridge.

'Perhaps we'll get the day off,' said Michael Ward.

'Shut up, Wardy,' said Chris.

Later, all the children went into the hall. Mr Saffrey looked upset. Everyone felt sorry for him.

'Well, you've all seen what's happened,' he said sadly. 'The roof is badly damaged. The missing tiles and lead can be replaced. It will cost a lot of money.'

Mr Saffrey sighed. 'I'm sorry about the copper cockerel. It has been stolen before. This time, we may never get it back.'

Chapter 4

Half term started badly for Kat and Arjo. Mrs Wilson looked cross. 'I'm sorry,' she said. 'I can't leave you and Arjo here all day. You will just have to come with me.'

Kat sighed. That was the trouble with her mum's job. She was a lorry driver. It meant she was away all day. Sometimes she was away for two or three days at a time.

Kat's mum and dad owned a firm called *Wilson Express*. They delivered goods all over the country. Mrs Wilson had her own lorry. It was a fourteen tonne truck.

If she could, Mrs Wilson only did short runs. Sometimes she had a long run. Then it was a problem.

It was worse in the school holidays. Then Mrs Wilson paid someone to look after Kat and Arjo.

'I'm on a long run tomorrow,' said Mrs Wilson. 'Dad won't be back. I can't get anyone to look after you. So I'm taking you both with me.'

Kat sighed again. She hated sitting for hours in her mum's lorry.

'Stop making a face,' said Mrs Wilson. 'You're coming with me and that's that.'

Chapter 5

They were on the road early. Kat still felt sleepy. Arjo was in the sleeping compartment above the cab. He was fast asleep.

Mrs Wilson was not in a good mood. She was worried about the cargo. 'I've never had to carry anything like it,' she said. 'I hope they don't move about. They could damage the lorry.'

'What have you got back there?' asked Kat.

'Lions,' said her mum.

Kat gasped.

'Two stone lions,' Mrs Wilson went on. 'They're in wooden crates. They're old. They came from a big house. They used to stand at the gates. They weigh about half a tonne. One of them hasn't got a front paw.'

'Where are you taking them?' asked Kat.

'To a place that sells things like stone lions,' said her mum.

'They get things from old houses,' went on Mrs Wilson. 'They sell old fireplaces, doors, old tiles, bricks, iron railings - anything.'

'How long will it take to get there?' asked Kat.

'A long time,' said Kat's mum with a grin. 'You'd better not get on my nerves, or I'll put you in with the lions.'

Kat laughed.

Chapter 6

It took three hours to get there. Kat
and Arjo felt bored. At last the lorry
turned off the motorway. 'Almost
there,' said Kat's mum.

The place looked a like an old junk
yard. It had a high fence round it.
Inside there were two big sheds.

Mrs Wilson drove through the
gates and stopped. She helped Kat
and Arjo out of the lorry. 'Have a
look round,' she said. 'But be careful.
I'll find out what to do about the
lions.' She went into one of the sheds.

In a corner of the yard was an old
iron swing. Arjo ran over and sat on
it. 'Push me, Kat,' he shouted.

There was a white transit van in the yard. Kat watched it while she pushed the swing. A man and a woman were unloading something.

They were taking old roof tiles out of the van.

The tiles were the sort that went along the ridge of a roof. Kat stared at them.

She had seen tiles like them before.

Chapter 7

Kat looked at the tiles closely. She had once done a drawing of the school. She had spent a long time drawing the roof. The tiles looked just like the ones that had been stolen.

Kat felt excited and nervous. What else was in the van? What if these people were the thieves? What if they had the copper cockerel?

Kat tried to sound calm. She spoke to Arjo. 'Let's have a look round,' she said. 'Come on.'

The doors of the van were open. All the tiles had been taken out. But lying at the back was a dirty old sheet. It was covering something.

Kat spoke slowly to Arjo. 'I'm going to look. Keep a lookout. I want to see what's under that old sheet.'

Arjo looked scared. He watched Kat crawl into the van. He saw her lift the corner of the sheet.

He couldn't believe his eyes. There was the copper cockerel. There was no mistaking it.

Chapter 8

After that, everything happened
quickly. The man and woman came
back. Arjo hadn't seen them coming.
He had been too busy looking into
the van.

The woman walked to the back of the van. Kat dived under the sheet. The woman shut the doors. She hardly noticed Arjo.

The man started the engine. The woman got into the van. Then they drove away.

At first Arjo couldn't do anything. He couldn't shout. He couldn't run. He just stood there frozen to the spot. Kat was in the van. She was being driven away from him. And it was his fault.

Then the van was out of sight. Arjo raced back to the sheds. He began to shout. 'They've taken Kat!' he screamed. 'They've taken Kat!'

He went on shouting. People ran out of one of the sheds. They stood round Arjo. Mrs Wilson bent down. She held him by the arms. 'Calm down. Tell me slowly,' she said.

Arjo told her about the van. He told her that Kat had found the copper cockerel in the back. 'Kat is still inside,' he said. 'You've got to stop them.'

29

Chapter 9

Mrs Wilson ran to the lorry and jumped inside. She pulled Arjo into it. 'Arjo,' she shouted. 'Which way did they go?'

Arjo pointed.

Mrs Wilson started the engine. The lorry roared across the yard and swung out of the gates.

Arjo had never known his mum drive fast. Now she raced down the road. She hoped to catch the van up, but it was too far ahead.

Arjo felt scared. The road was quite narrow and bumpy. He felt himself being thrown from side to side. 'Slow down, Mum,' he shouted.

'Just hold tight,' Mrs Wilson
shouted back.

At last they saw the van just ahead.
It turned on to the motorway and
sped down the slip road. The lorry
followed.

32

Mrs Wilson began to catch up with the van. Soon she was right behind it. She turned on her lights and pressed the horn. The van didn't slow down. Instead it went faster.

'Why won't they pull over?' gasped Mrs Wilson.

Chapter 10

Mrs Wilson had a phone in the cab.
She pressed 999 and asked for the
police. She told them she was on the
motorway.

'This is Wilson Express,' she said. 'I'm ten miles from Junction 9 – heading south. I'm behind a white van. My daughter is trapped inside it. The van may have stolen goods.'

'Please wait,' said a voice. 'We will contact the motorway police.'

After a while, the voice spoke again. 'The motorway police are on their way,' it said. 'They'll go straight to Junction 8.'

Mrs Wilson gritted her teeth. Junction 8 was some distance away. Then she had another idea.

In the lorry she had a CB radio. Most big lorries have them. Sometimes, lorry drivers use them to talk to each other. They can pass on news. They can warn each other of hold-ups on the road.

Mrs Wilson turned the CB radio on. She spoke into it. 'I need help,' she said. 'I need it urgently. My daughter is in danger. Please respond if you can help.'

Chapter 11

Kat was terrified. She didn't move.

The van driver looked in his mirror. 'That lorry is still there,' said the man. 'I can't shake it off.'

The lorry was behind them. Its lights were on full beam.

'Why is it chasing us?' asked the woman.

'I don't know,' said the man. 'But I don't like it.'

'Can't you go any faster?' said the woman.

'Yes,' said the man. 'I'll put my foot down.'

There was a line of lorries ahead.
Suddenly one of them pulled across
to the outside lane. 'Hey,' shouted the
man. 'What's he doing? That's
against the law.'

Then the lorries slowed down.
They closed in on the van. Soon, the
van was boxed in.

'We're in a trap,' shouted the man. 'What do they want?'

The lorries turned off the motorway. They forced the van to turn off, too. They drove into a service area. Then they slowed to a stop.

The man leaped out of the van. The lorry drivers jumped down from their cabs. The man tried to run, but he was blocked in.

The woman in the van didn't move.

In the distance was the wail of a police siren.

Chapter 12

Mrs Wilson ran to the van. She pulled open the back doors.

Kat was still lying under the old sheet. She was shaking.

'It's all right, Kat,' said Mrs Wilson. 'You're safe now.'

Kat climbed out. Arjo looked at Kat. His eyes looked bigger than ever. 'I was so scared,' he said. He gave Kat a huge hug.

Mrs Wilson pulled back the sheet. 'You were right, Arjo,' she gasped. 'I just can't believe it. This is the copper cockerel. I'd know it anywhere. This is the second time we've rescued it.'

A police officer spoke to Mrs Wilson. 'Perhaps you'll tell us what this is all about,' he said. 'It sounded urgent.'

Mrs Wilson pointed at the white van. 'There are stolen goods in there,' she said.

'Can you prove that?' asked the police officer.

'We think we can,' said Kat.

'Well, I hope so,' said the police officer.

Chapter 13

Kat told the police officer everything. He wrote it all down in his notebook. It took a long time.

In the end, the police officer let the man and woman go.

'Why didn't they arrest them?' asked Kat.

'They'll have to prove the cockerel was stolen,' said Mrs Wilson. 'Mr Saffrey can do that.'

The police took the copper cockerel out of the van. They put it in the back of their car. It didn't quite fit in. Part of it poked through the back window.

'We'll let you know what's happening as soon as we can,' said the police officer.

Then he looked sternly at Mrs Wilson. 'Boxing in that van was a risky thing to do.'

'I know,' said Mrs Wilson, 'but Kat was inside it.'

The officer turned to Kat. 'I know you wanted to help,' he said, 'but getting into a strange van was dangerous. Don't ever do a thing like that again.'

'Don't worry. I won't,' said Kat. 'I was so scared.'

Arjo sighed. 'Can we go home now?' he said. 'I'm hungry.'

Mrs Wilson pointed at her lorry. 'I'm afraid not,' she said. 'I've still got two stone lions to deliver.'